This book belongs to

Shravya

The
EVERYDAY
WORKINGS
of MACHINES

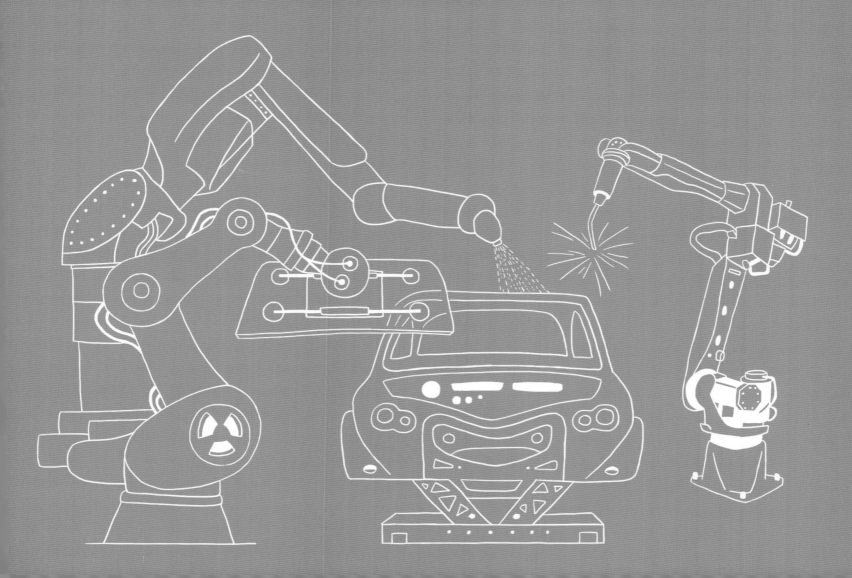

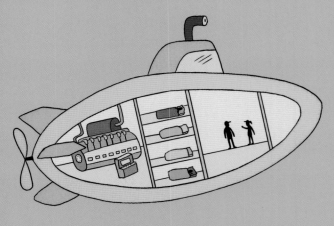
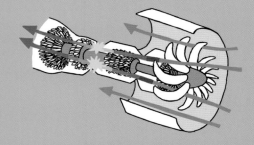
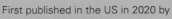
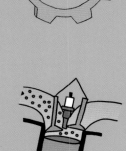

First published in the US in 2020 by

Ivy Kids

An imprint of The Quarto Group
Quarto Boston North Shore
100 Cummings Center, Suite 265D
Beverly, MA 01915, USA
Tel: +1 978-282-9590, Fax: +1 978-283-2742
www.QuartoKnows.com

A CIP record for this book is available
from the Library of Congress.

ISBN: 978-0-7112-5427-5

This book was conceived, designed, & produced by

Ivy Kids

58 West Street, Brighton BN1 2RA, United Kingdom

PUBLISHER Georgia Amson-Bradshaw
MANAGING EDITOR Susie Behar
ART DIRECTORS Kate Haynes & Hanri van Wyk
PROJECT EDITOR Cath Senker
DESIGNER Emily Portnoi
EDITORS Hannah Dove & Lucy Menzies

Printed in China TT052021

3 5 7 9 10 8 6 4 2

MIX
Paper from
responsible sources
FSC
www.fsc.org
FSC® C016973

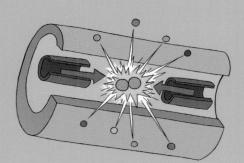

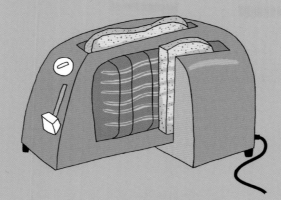

The
EVERYDAY
WORKINGS
of MACHINES

How machines work,
from toasters and trains
to hovercrafts and robots

Steve martin

illustrated by Valpuri Kerttula

IVY KIDS

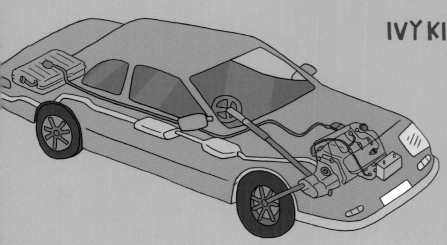

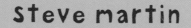

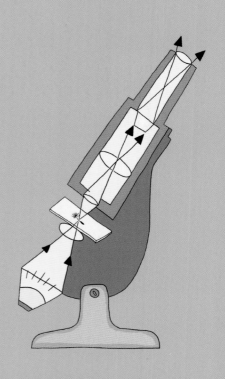

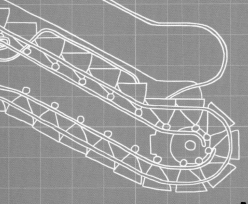

CONTENTS

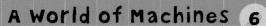

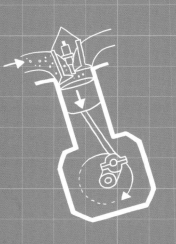

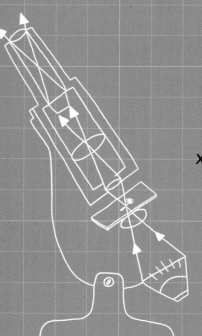

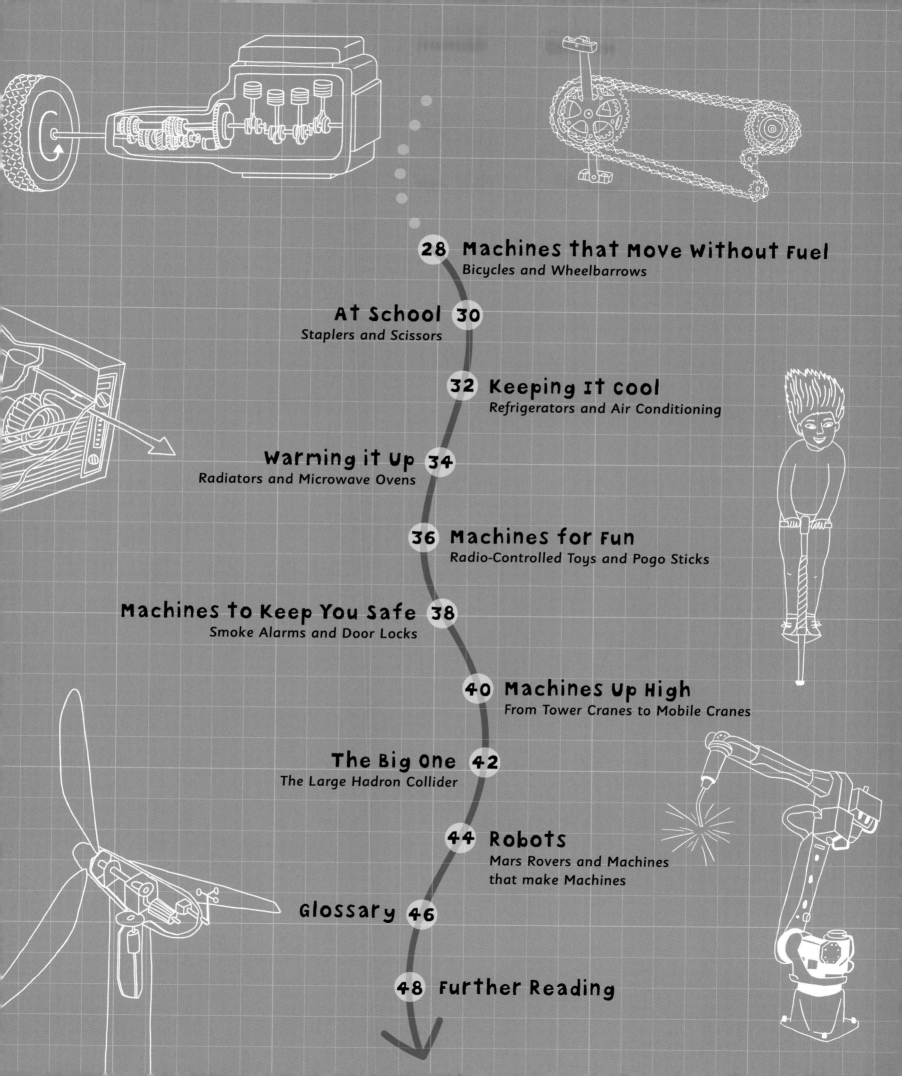

A WORLD OF MACHINES

Machines have been around since the first humans, from pieces of flint that were used to break or cut things, to the invention of the wheel. You might use hundreds of machines every day!

Imagine this ... You bounce out of bed and into the bathroom. You flush the toilet (we hope!) and have a nice hot shower. It's breakfast time—you pop bread into the toaster and grab a cold drink from the refrigerator. Time to go to school, so you lock the front door, hop on your bike, and you're off. In just an hour or so you have used multiple machines. Can you count how many?

We use so many machines because they make our lives easier. They help us to do work. In science, "work" means getting things done, and machines let us get things done using less effort.

In this book, you'll find out how all kinds of machines work, from the simple wheelbarrow to the high-tech robots exploring Mars. You'll never look at machines in the same way again!

Simple machines

There are different types of machines: simple machines (made up of a few parts) and compound machines (made up of lots of different simple machines). A pair of scissors, for example, is made up of levers (the handles) and wedges (the blades). Here's how some simple machines work.

Wedge

A wedge has a thick and a thin end. If you push it in one direction, it makes a force in a sideways direction. This makes it useful for splitting or separating objects. The blades of a pair of scissors are wedges. When you push them through paper, they cut it into two pieces.

Lever

A lever is a bar that rests on a fixed point called a fulcrum. It reduces the effort or force needed to move or lift a heavy object. A wheelbarrow is made up of multiple simple machines, including a lever—its wheel is the fulcrum and its handles are the bars. You raise the handles of a wheelbarrow to lift the heavy load in the barrow.

Pulley

A pulley is a wheel with a rope looped around its edge. It makes it easier to lift things. By pulling down on one side of the rope, you can turn the wheel and lift the object at the other end. Cranes use pulleys to lift heavy loads.

Wheel and axle

An axle is a rod that is fixed to the middle of a wheel. A car axle has a wheel fixed to both ends. When force is applied to the axle, the wheels turn.

HOUSEHOLD MACHINES

Your house is packed with machines. Arguably, two of the most important are the toaster, because toast is the best, and the toilet, because ... well, you know why. But have you ever wondered how these household machines work? Let's take a look at them in more detail.

Toaster

Some machines turn electricity into heat. This is how a toaster turns cold, soft bread into hot, crunchy toast.

1 You slide a slice of bread in the toaster.

2 You press the lever down. This lowers the bread down and also completes a circuit that allows electricity to flow through the wires. These wires are in rows on either side of the bread.

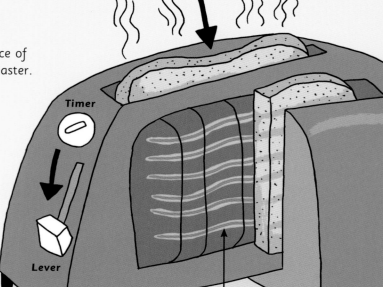

Bread goes down

Timer

Lever

Wires

3 The electricity doesn't flow through the wires very easily, so they turn red hot. The heat from the wires then cooks the bread until it turns brown.

4 The toaster is on a timer. When the toast has cooked for the right amount of time, the lever is released, breaking the circuit. The toast pops up, ready for a topping of your choice.

Toast pops up

GOOD AND BAD CONDUCTORS

Most electrical wires are made from copper because it is a good conductor. This means electricity flows through the wires easily. But wires made from poor conductors are also useful. When electricity flows through them, they become hot. The wires in a toaster are usually made from nichrome, a poor conductor.

Toilet

You go to the toilet. Then you press a button or handle, and water comes to flush away your pee or poop. How does it work?

HINT: It's not a toilet fairy!

1

Water for flushing the toilet is held in a tank called a cistern. The flush handle is a lever, and when you press it, it opens a valve (a small door), which lets the water rush out of the cistern and into the toilet bowl.

Cistern

Lever

Water is released from the cistern to the toilet bowl.

Valve opens

Toilet bowl

2

The flowing water forces the waste and water in the toilet bowl into the waste pipe, which leads to the main drain. Farewell, poop! As the cistern empties, the ballcock floating on the water moves down.

Valve opens and fresh water rushes in.

Ballcock moves down

Valve closes

Waste pipe

3

When the cistern is empty two things happen: 1. the valve closes, 2. the ballcock reaches the bottom and pushes a lever that opens a second valve at the bottom of the cistern to let in fresh water from the main water supply.

Valve closes

Ballcock rises back up

4

As the water level rises, the ballcock also rises. When it reaches the right level, the valve closes and water stops flowing in. Your toilet is now clean and ready for its next visitor!

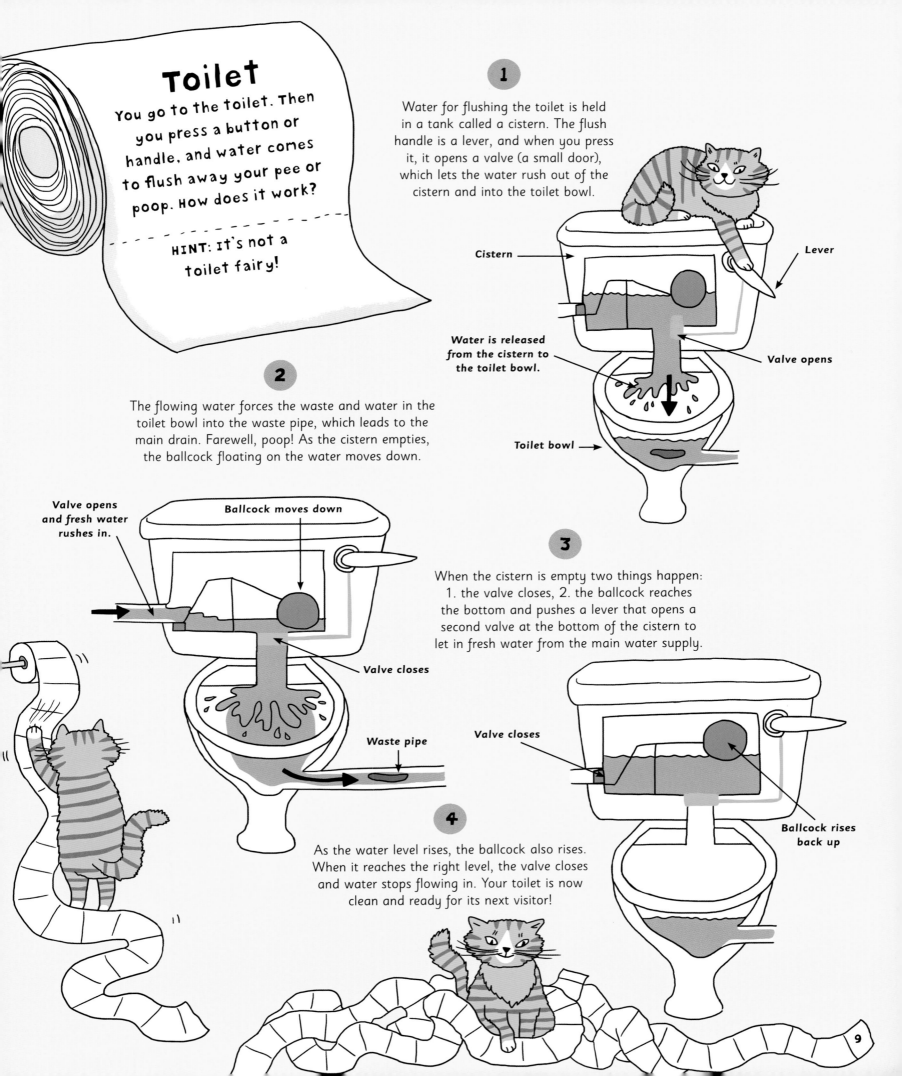

AT THE MALL

Malls are teeming with useful machines. Escalators help you get around quickly without tiring you out, while barcode scanners help stores sell and keep track of their items. Let's give these everyday machines some attention!

Escalator

An escalator takes up no more room than a staircase but can move far more people, far more quickly. And it saves them having to climb stairs! But how does it work?

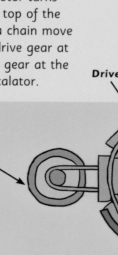

The shortest escalator in the world is in Japan. It's about 32 inches long and has only 5 steps!

1

Firstly, an electric motor turns the drive gear at the top of the escalator. This makes a chain move in a loop around the drive gear at the top and the return gear at the bottom of the escalator.

2

As it moves, the chain pulls along a series of steps which carry people up or down. Each step rests against the next as they move.

3

At the top and bottom of the escalator, the steps collapse on each other and flatten out. This makes a flat surface that is easy and safe for people to walk on.

4

While the chain is turning and pulling the steps, the handrail is also moving. Like the drive gear, the handrail drive is turned by the electric motor and makes the handrail move in a loop. The handrail moves at the same speed as the steps. Handy!

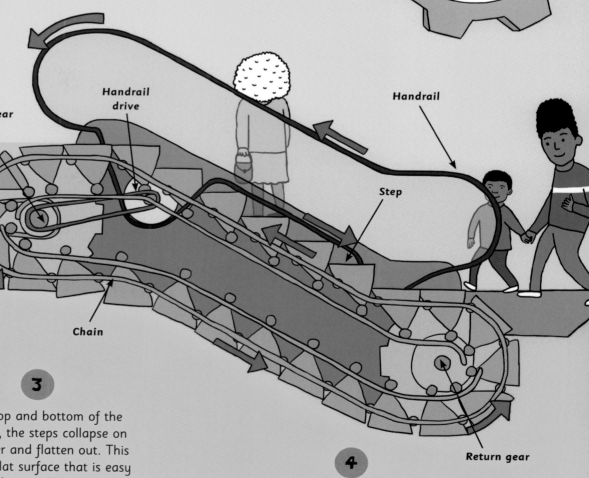

Drive gear

Handrail drive

Handrail

Electric motor

Step

Chain

Return gear

Barcode scanner

Blip ... Blip ... Blip! It's checkout time and the scanner is working away reading all the barcodes. Find out how it works.

1 Yay! You've finally found the perfect pair of jeans. You take them to the checkout and hand them to the sales clerk. Like every other item in the store, the jeans have their very own barcode.

2 The sales clerk uses a machine called a scanner to shine a light over the barcode. The white stripes reflect light back and the black lines do not. A sensor inside the scanner detects the pattern of the reflected light and creates a matching signal.

3 An electric circuit inside the scanner converts the signal into binary (the language that computers work in) and sends this to a computer. The computer identifies the code and matches it to the item. It shows what it is, how much it costs, and how many are left in stock. You got the last pair—good work!

WHAT IS A BARCODE?

You'll have seen black-and-white barcode stripes on most products in your shopping cart, from toothpaste to chocolate. Together with scanners and a computer, they help store owners keep track of sales.

Barcodes are made up of a series of numbers. Numbers are easy to mix up though. For example, a 6 could be read upside down as a 9. For this reason, the numbers appear as a code. The code works by giving each number seven randomly ordered, black-and-white stripes.

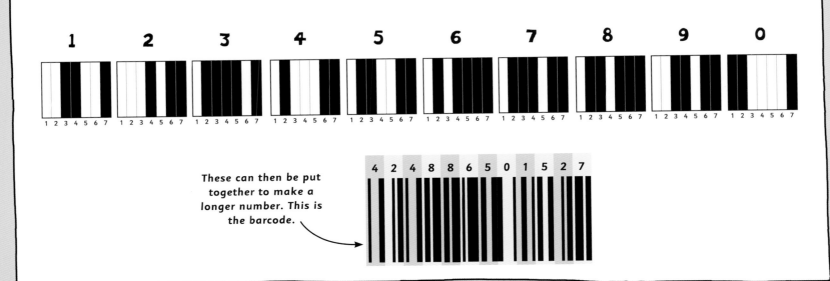

1 2 3 4 5 6 7 8 9 0

These can then be put together to make a longer number. This is the barcode.

4 2 4 8 8 6 5 0 1 5 2 7

THE CAR

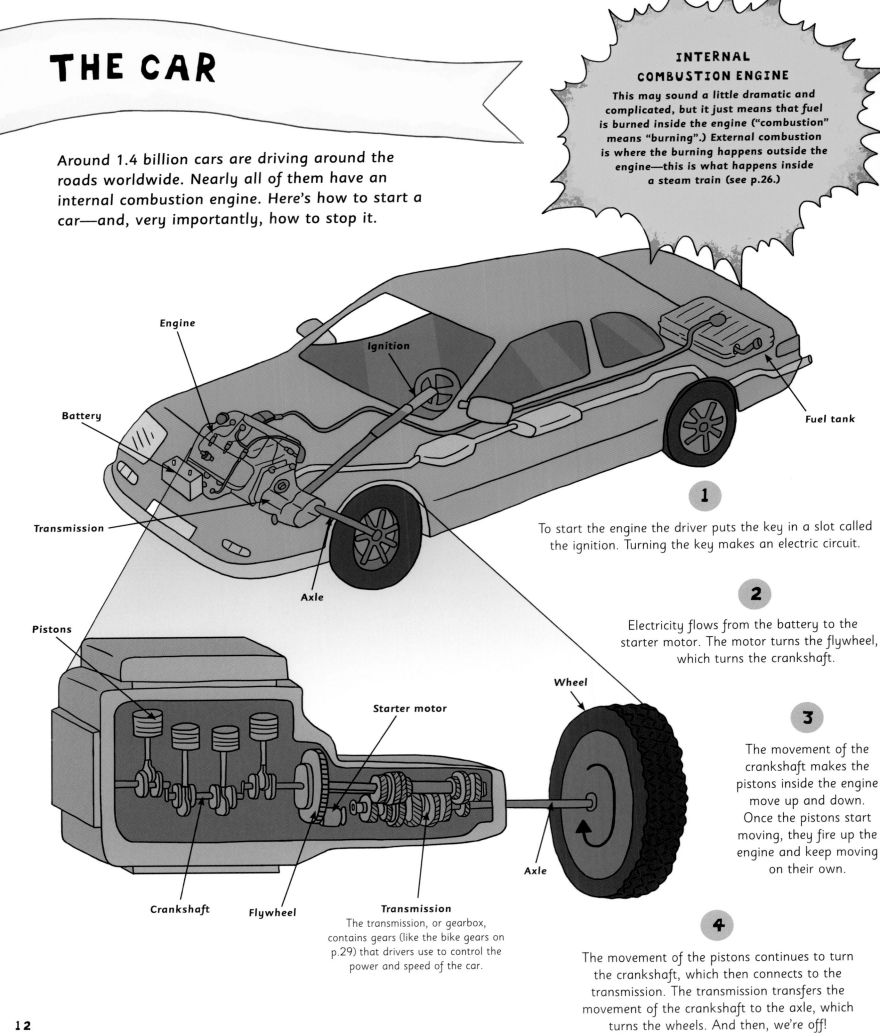

Around 1.4 billion cars are driving around the roads worldwide. Nearly all of them have an internal combustion engine. Here's how to start a car—and, very importantly, how to stop it.

Engine

Ignition

Battery

Fuel tank

Transmission

Axle

Pistons

Wheel

Starter motor

Axle

Crankshaft   Flywheel

Transmission
The transmission, or gearbox, contains gears (like the bike gears on p.29) that drivers use to control the power and speed of the car.

1
To start the engine the driver puts the key in a slot called the ignition. Turning the key makes an electric circuit.

2
Electricity flows from the battery to the starter motor. The motor turns the flywheel, which turns the crankshaft.

3
The movement of the crankshaft makes the pistons inside the engine move up and down. Once the pistons start moving, they fire up the engine and keep moving on their own.

4
The movement of the pistons continues to turn the crankshaft, which then connects to the transmission. The transmission transfers the movement of the crankshaft to the axle, which turns the wheels. And then, we're off!

Pistons

But wait a minute ... how do pistons keep moving on their own?

1

The turning crankshaft causes the piston to move down when the car is started. Fuel from the fuel tank, mixed with air, now enters the cylinder (the tube the piston sits inside of).

2

When the piston moves back up, the fuel and air mixture is squeezed into a small space.

3

A spark plug sets fire to the fuel and air mixture, which then explodes and pushes the piston down again.

4

When the piston comes back up, it pushes all the exhaust fumes (waste gases) out. The process then begins again with each explosion now creating the movement of the piston.

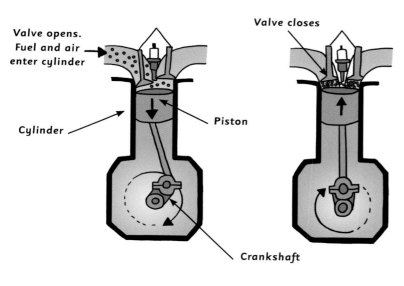

Valve opens. Fuel and air enter cylinder

Cylinder

Piston

Crankshaft

Valve closes

Spark plug

Explosion

Valve opens and waste gases go out

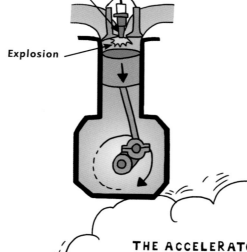

THE ACCELERATOR

To go faster, drivers use the accelerator pedal. When they press it, more air enters the cylinders in the engine. This causes more fuel to be added and more explosions, making the pistons move faster.

Hit the brakes!

To stop or slow a car, a driver presses a brake pedal with their foot. Car brakes are quite similar to the brakes on a bike (see p.29).

1 Woah, a herd of cows is on the road! The driver presses the brake pedal, which pushes a lever.

2 The lever pushes a piston, which then pushes brake fluid down a narrow pipe.

3 The fluid reaches a second piston, which presses the brake pads against a disk on the wheel.

4 The friction between the pad and the disk slows down the wheel and stops the car. The cows are safe to moo another day!

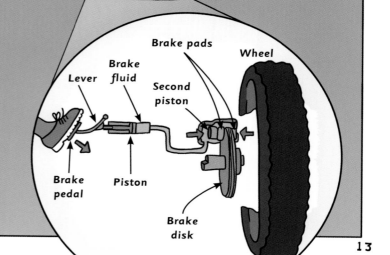

Lever

Brake fluid

Brake pads

Wheel

Second piston

Brake pedal

Piston

Brake disk

IN THE AIR

When you're sat on plane, traveling to an exciting destination, it's easy to take it for granted. But isn't it amazing that these heavy machines fly through the air like birds? Engines move a plane forward, while the wings move it upward. See how...

Tail fin

Tail plane

Overhead storage

Fuselage

Ailerons
These wing flaps move up and down to make the plane turn left or right.

Luggage compartment

Emergency exit

Engine
Large planes have four engines.

Wings

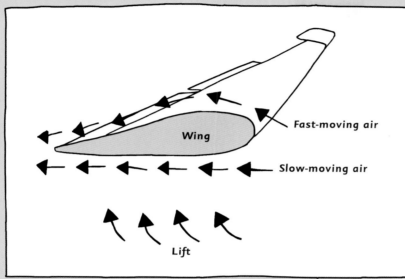

Fast-moving air

Wing

Slow-moving air

Lift

A plane's engines move it forward at high speed. This makes air flow rapidly over the wings. The wings are shaped so that the air moving over the top of the wing travels faster than the air beneath the wing. The fast-moving air above has less pressure than the air below. This creates a force called lift, which pushes the plane upward into the air. The angle of the wing pushes air downward, and this also creates lift.

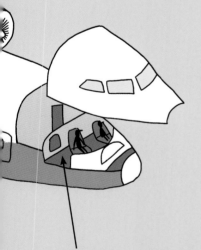

Wing

Cockpit
The pilot and co-pilot sit here and use controls inside the cockpit to fly the plane.

Engines

1
Planes use jet engines, which suck air into the engine through a fan.

2
Rotating blades (called a compressor) force the air into a smaller and smaller space. This squeezes the air to a very high pressure.

3
This hot, high-pressure air reaches the combustion chamber, where it is mixed with fuel, and a spark lights the fuel/air mixture.

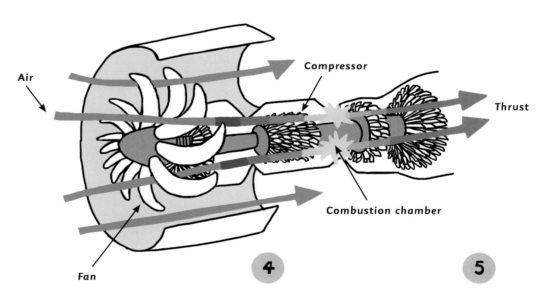

Air

Compressor

Thrust

Combustion chamber

Fan

4
This makes the fuel/air mixture expand very quickly and blast out of the back of the engine.

5
The force of this backward blast pushes the plane forward. This force is called thrust.

OVER AND UNDER THE SEA

Ships sail on the sea. But other machines can speed along over and under the water. A hovercraft glides above the waves, while a submarine can sink down deep beneath them.

Hovercraft

A hovercraft may look like it's sailing on the water but actually, it's gliding on air. How? Take a look!

Rear fans

Air blows backward and makes the hovercraft move forward.

Fan

Air blows downward, filling the rubber skirt and creating an air cushion.

1

A large, powerful fan pushes air down through the hovercraft.

2

The skirt under the hovercraft traps the air, making a huge cushion. The air cushion pushes the hovercraft up off the surface. This reduces the friction between the hovercraft and the water, which allows the hovercraft to move more easily.

3

Fans at the back of the hovercraft blow air backward to make it move forward. It's like when you blow up a balloon and let it go—the air rushing out makes it fly away.

FRICTION

Friction is a force between two surfaces or objects that are sliding against each other. The more friction, the slower and harder it is to move. Surfaces such as ice have less friction so you can move (or slip!) on them easily.

Submarine

If an object is lighter than water it floats, and if it is heavier than water, it sinks. A submarine works by changing its weight so that it can do both.

Argh, the Kraken!

Propeller

Outer hull

Inner hull

Ballast tank

1

A submarine is made up of an outer hull and an inner hull with gaps between the hulls known as the ballast tanks. The crew stay warm and dry inside the inner hull. A propeller at the back of the submarine drives it forward.

Ballast tank

Air out

Inner hull

Outer hull

Water in

Air in

Water out

2

When the submarine needs to dive down under the water, the crew lets water into the ballast tanks. This forces air out of the submarine and as it takes on more water and more weight, it sinks. The crew can control how deep the submarine goes by changing the amount of water in the tanks.

3

When the submarine needs to rise back up to the surface, the crew blasts air into the ballast tanks, which forces the water back out. The submarine becomes lighter and rises up.

LIFE ON A SUBMARINE

Oxygen is pumped into the submarine so that the crew can breathe.

Submarines also have special machines that can turn saltwater into fresh water so that the crew have a constant supply of drinking water.

17

MACHINES THAT TURN

Fossil fuels (coal, oil, and gas) are very bad for the planet and will run out one day, so scientists and engineers have been developing machines that make electricity using sources that never run out, like wind and waves. That's where turbines come in.

Wind turbine

These giant machines create electricity using the power of wind, which will never run out! And they cause much less pollution and harm to our world. Find out more about these planet-saving machines ...

Wind turbines are often built on high, flat land or even out in the ocean. This is because there are no buildings or hills to slow the wind down in these open spaces. That means the turbines face more powerful winds and can make more electricity.

Tidal turbine

These turbines are like underwater windmills, but instead of harnessing the wind they use the motion of the tides.

Tidal turbines are placed underwater and fixed to the seabed. The natural movement of the water, caused by tides, makes the blades rotate and generate electricity.

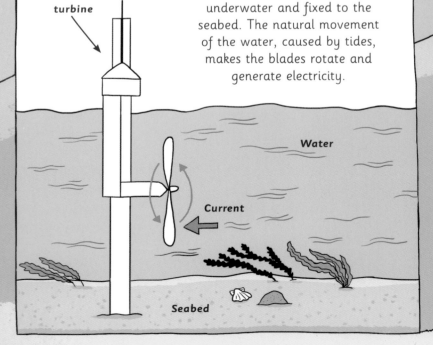

Tidal turbine

Water

Current

Seabed

Most wind turbines are more than 300 feet tall. They're made this tall because wind speed increases with height. For example, at 120-feet high, the wind is twice as fast as on the ground. The faster the wind, the more the turbine's blades will turn, and the more electricity will be made.

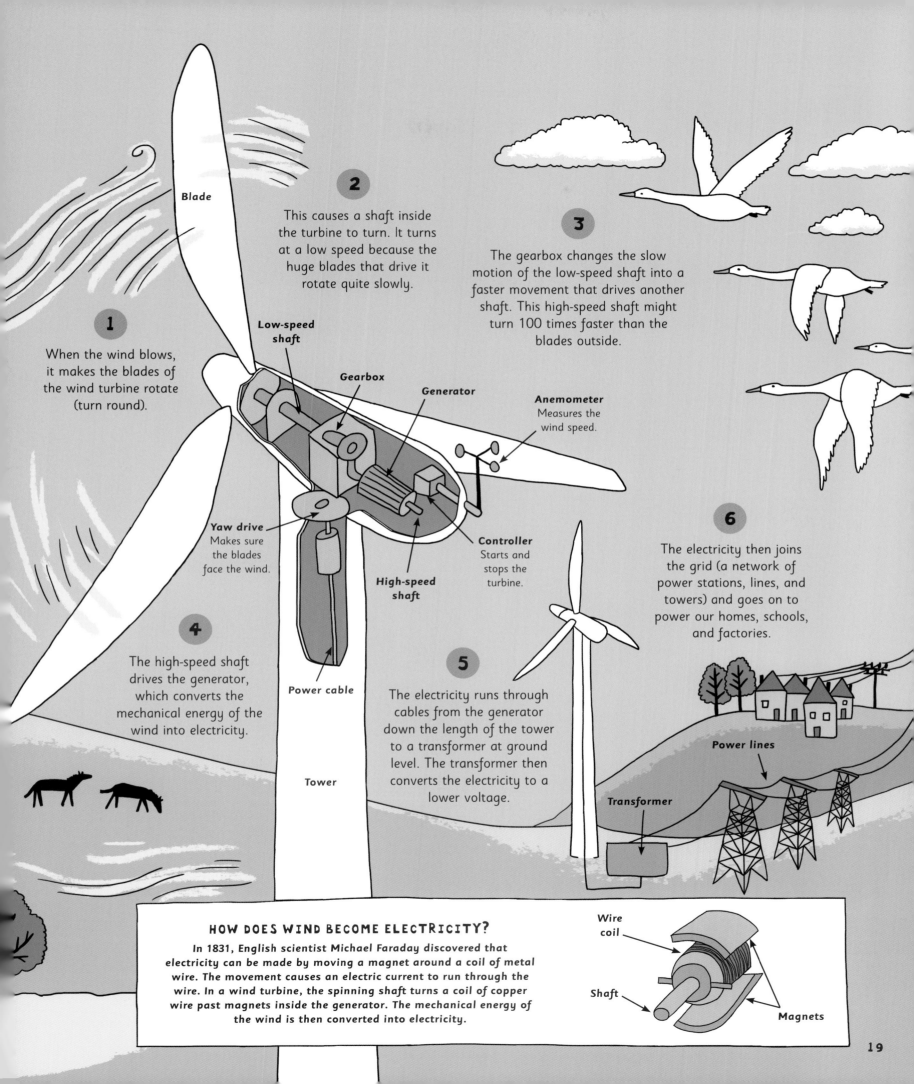

Blade

2 This causes a shaft inside the turbine to turn. It turns at a low speed because the huge blades that drive it rotate quite slowly.

3 The gearbox changes the slow motion of the low-speed shaft into a faster movement that drives another shaft. This high-speed shaft might turn 100 times faster than the blades outside.

1 When the wind blows, it makes the blades of the wind turbine rotate (turn round).

Low-speed shaft

Gearbox

Generator

Anemometer
Measures the wind speed.

Yaw drive
Makes sure the blades face the wind.

High-speed shaft

Controller
Starts and stops the turbine.

6 The electricity then joins the grid (a network of power stations, lines, and towers) and goes on to power our homes, schools, and factories.

4 The high-speed shaft drives the generator, which converts the mechanical energy of the wind into electricity.

Power cable

Tower

5 The electricity runs through cables from the generator down the length of the tower to a transformer at ground level. The transformer then converts the electricity to a lower voltage.

Power lines

Transformer

HOW DOES WIND BECOME ELECTRICITY?

In 1831, English scientist Michael Faraday discovered that electricity can be made by moving a magnet around a coil of metal wire. The movement causes an electric current to run through the wire. In a wind turbine, the spinning shaft turns a coil of copper wire past magnets inside the generator. The mechanical energy of the wind is then converted into electricity.

Wire coil

Shaft

Magnets

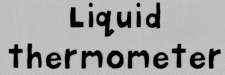

Every day we use machines to measure things: checking the temperature so we know whether to wrap up warm, or weighing ingredients for a delicious home-baked cake. Do you know how these helpful machines work?

Liquid thermometer

These simple thermometers have been around for more than 300 years.

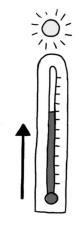

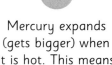

1
You wake up and wonder how cold it is outside, so you check the temperature on a thermometer. This thermometer is a glass tube filled with a liquid. The liquid is usually mercury, which is a liquid metal.

2
Mercury expands (gets bigger) when it is hot. This means that, as it gets warm, the liquid is pushed up the tube. The line on the thermometer will tell you what the temperature is.

3
Mercury contracts (gets smaller) when it is cold. This means that, as it gets cold, the liquid goes down in the tube. Hmm, it might not be a barbecue day!

DANIEL GABRIEL FAHRENHEIT (1686-1736) AND ANDERS CELSIUS (1701-1744)

Daniel Gabriel Fahrenheit was a German physicist who invented the first mercury thermometer in 1714. Ten years later, he introduced the world to the temperature scale still used in the US today. It was named the Fahrenheit scale after its inventor. On the Fahrenheit scale, the freezing point of water is 32°F and the boiling point is 212°F.

This is not the only temperature scale, though. In 1742, nearly 20 years after Fahrenheit's scale, a Swedish astronomer named Anders Celsius came up with another scale. In the Celsius scale, water freezes at 0°C and boils at 100°C. Today, most countries in the world use the Celsius system.

FAHRENHEIT

CELSIUS

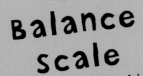

Balance Scale

This simple weighing machine has been around since the days of the Ancient Egyptians.

1

You want to find out the weight of three apples. You place the apples on one side of the scale.

2

You place weights on the other side. You take off and add the weights until the two sides of the scale are balanced.

3

To find the weight of the apples, you just need to practice your math and add up the weights. Easy peasy!

$$100g + 50g + 20g = 170g$$

Electronic thermometer

If you're sick, this is probably the kind of thermometer you'll use.

1

An electronic thermometer works on the principle that the hotter a metal becomes, the more difficult it is for electricity to flow through it. So, when the metal bit of the thermometer is placed under your tongue, the metal heats up and the flow of electricity changes.

100° F

2

A microchip records the amount of electricity flowing through the metal and converts it into a temperature reading on the screen. Yes, you've got a fever. It's a day in bed for you!

MACHINES TO HELP YOU SEE

Our eyes allow us to see the world around us, close up and far away. But we can't see inside solid objects or tiny things smaller than a pinprick. X-ray machines and microscopes make it possible.

X-ray machine

An X-ray is a type of light ray but it is invisible. Imagine your friend Sara has fallen off her bike and hurt her arm. At the hospital she can have an X-ray so that the doctors can see the bones in her arm and check if they are broken.

X-ray tube

X-rays

Detector

1

The X-ray machine is pointed at Sara's arm. The operator presses a button, and X-ray beams travel through the air.

2

The X-rays pass through the soft parts in Sara's arm—the skin and muscles—but they cannot pass through the hard bones. The bones block the X-ray and make a shadow on the other side. It's like when you shine a flashlight on your hand, and it makes a shadow behind it.

3

On the other side of Sara's arm, the detector creates an image.

4

The detector is linked to a computer. On the screen, the soft body parts show up as black or gray areas. The harder bones show up white. This lets the doctors see if they are broken. Poor Sara—her arm is broken after all!

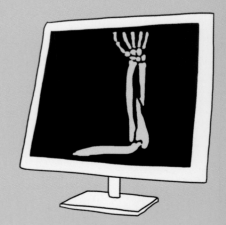

Microscope

Have you ever used a microscope? Microscopes allow you to see things you cannot normally see. You can examine tiny objects, insects, or even your own skin. Scientists use microscopes to study cells, invent medicines, make electronic materials, and much more. Let's see how they work.

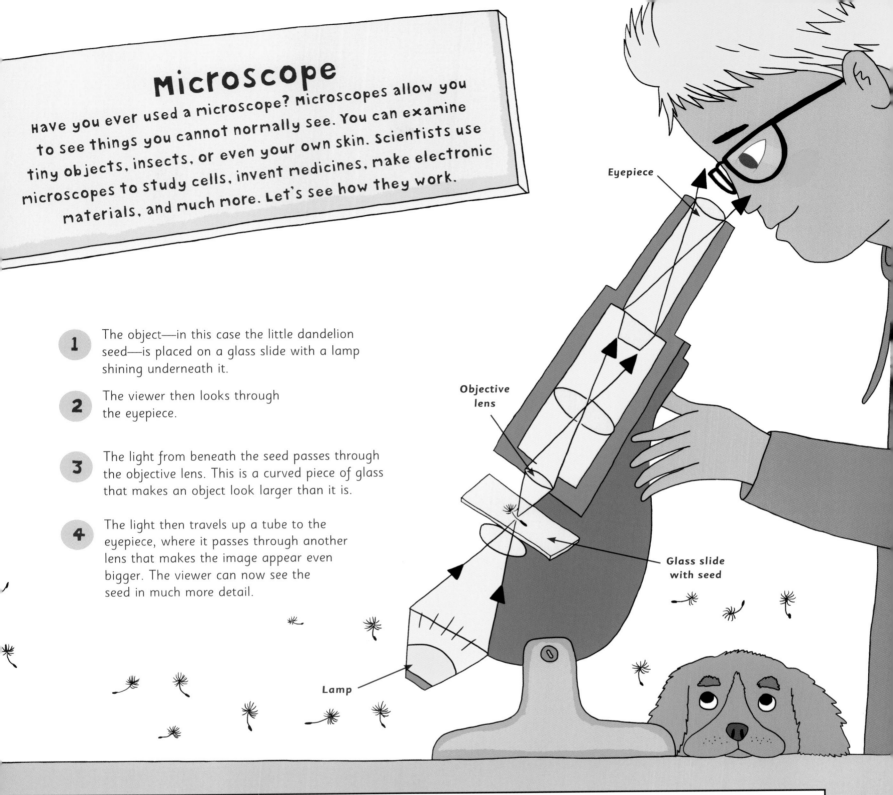

1 The object—in this case the little dandelion seed—is placed on a glass slide with a lamp shining underneath it.

2 The viewer then looks through the eyepiece.

3 The light from beneath the seed passes through the objective lens. This is a curved piece of glass that makes an object look larger than it is.

4 The light then travels up a tube to the eyepiece, where it passes through another lens that makes the image appear even bigger. The viewer can now see the seed in much more detail.

Eyepiece

Objective lens

Glass slide with seed

Lamp

HOW DO LENSES MAKE THE IMAGE BIGGER?

When light waves pass through a curved lens, the light passing through the sides of the lens bends more than the light passing through the center. This makes the light spread out when it passes through the lens and so the image appears bigger.

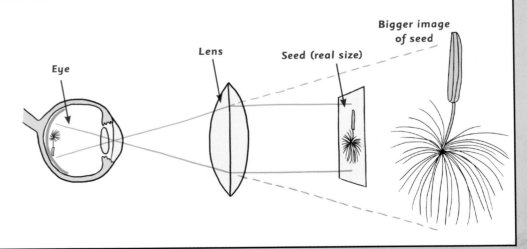

Eye

Lens

Seed (real size)

Bigger image of seed

SOUND

Microphones and cell phones allow you to hear what someone is saying or singing even if you're a long way away. That's because they turn sound waves into electrical signals that can travel great distances.

Microphone and Speaker

Singers use microphones and speakers so that the audience can hear them loud and clear. How do these machines work together?

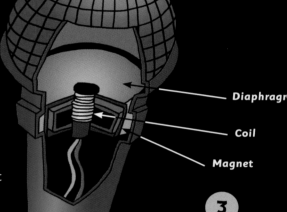

Microphone
Diaphragm
Coil
Magnet

1
It's karaoke night and your dad takes to the stage. When he starts belting out a song, his voice makes the air vibrate. This creates sound waves.

2
The sound waves enter the microphone and hit a diaphragm (disk), which vibrates with the movement of the sound waves.

3
When the diaphragm vibrates, so do a coil of wire and a magnet behind it. When the magnet moves against the wire, the wire becomes electrified. The vibration produces electrical signals that move in the same pattern as the sound waves.

4
The electrical signals travel from the microphone to the amplifier. The amplifier increases the voltage (electrical force) to make the signals more powerful.

Amplifier

Speaker

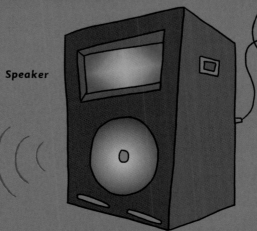

5
The electrical signals pass to the speaker, which changes them back into sound waves and sends them out—but much louder—to you in the crowd!

24

cell phone

You can pick up your phone and talk to your friend from school, your cousin across the country, or your grandpa on the opposite side of the world. How does your voice travel to their phone, and how does it happen so fast?

2

A microchip (mini-computer) inside your phone turns the signal into digital code—a series of numbers. The antenna then sends this code out into the air as radio waves, which travel to the nearest cell tower.

Cell tower

1

Say you're talking on the phone to your cousin in another town. The sound waves you make enter the microphone, which copies their pattern into a matching electrical signal.

3

The cell tower picks up the signal and passes it on to the base station.

Base station

4

The base station is linked to the Mobile Telephone Switching Office, or MTSO. This is a large computer that connects base stations from different areas. The MTSO works out the fastest way to pass on your call and sends this information back to the base station.

MTSO

5

The base station isn't powerful enough to send the radio waves all the way across the country. So it sends the radio waves through a series of cells—small areas that have at least one cell tower and base station—until they reach the nearest tower to your cousin.

Inside a phone

Antenna

Microchip

Microphone

6

The radio waves travel to your cousin's phone. The speaker in a phone is like a microphone in reverse. It turns the digital signal back into sound, and your cousin can hear your words!

TRAINS
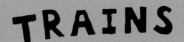

When people drive a car, they can choose which way to go, but train drivers have to follow the track. Trains get their energy in different ways. In the past, they used steam power, but nowadays, most trains run on electricity.

Steam train

The first steam trains were invented in the 1800s. They changed the way we moved materials and people from place to place. These trains could travel at up to 60 mph—the fastest humans had ever gone before. And they were all powered by steam!

1
Choo choo! A steam train is like a giant kettle on wheels. To get it chugging along, coal or sometimes wood is shoveled into a fire to keep it burning. This fire heats a huge tank of water.

Steam

Water tank

Coal

Cylinder

Crankshaft

Piston

2
The boiling water gives off steam, which pushes a piston inside a cylinder.

3
The piston is joined to a crankshaft that turns the wheels. Full steam ahead!

Electric train

Electric trains are powered by ... electricity, of course! They get the electricity either from an overhead cable or from a third rail that runs between the two rails that the wheels run on. This electricity powers the motors, which move the wheels. Take a closer look.

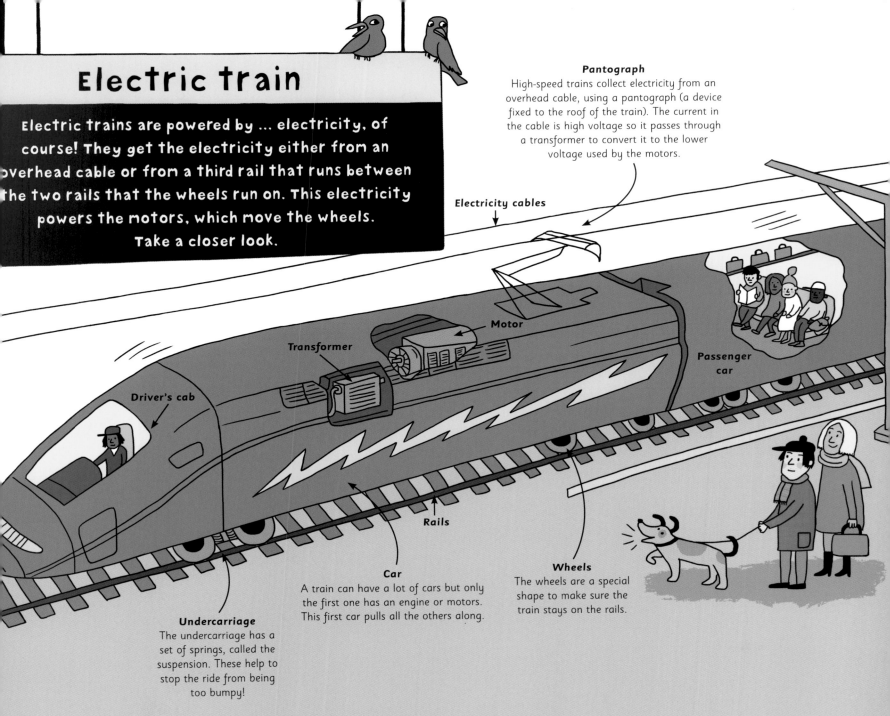

Pantograph
High-speed trains collect electricity from an overhead cable, using a pantograph (a device fixed to the roof of the train). The current in the cable is high voltage so it passes through a transformer to convert it to the lower voltage used by the motors.

Electricity cables

Motor

Transformer

Passenger car

Driver's cab

Rails

Car
A train can have a lot of cars but only the first one has an engine or motors. This first car pulls all the others along.

Wheels
The wheels are a special shape to make sure the train stays on the rails.

Undercarriage
The undercarriage has a set of springs, called the suspension. These help to stop the ride from being too bumpy!

STAYING ON TRACK

Trains get to their destinations by following a track. The wheels move along steel rails that are fastened on top of wooden blocks known as sleepers—together they form the track. The rails need to be exactly the same distance apart as the train's wheels. This distance is called the gauge. When the train needs to move onto another line, switches are used.

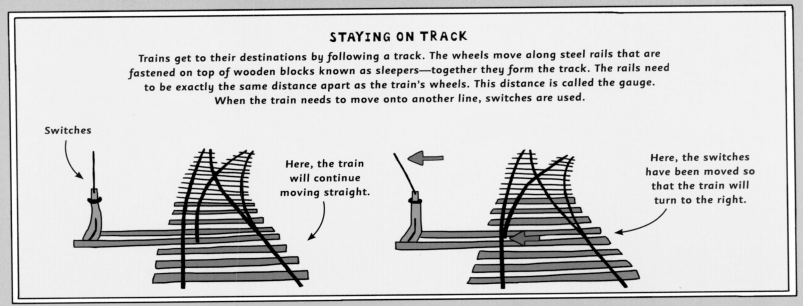

Switches

Here, the train will continue moving straight.

Here, the switches have been moved so that the train will turn to the right.

MACHINES THAT MOVE WITHOUT FUEL

You've probably ridden a bike before and enjoyed the whoosh of the wind on your face. And you've likely seen a wheelbarrow. But do you know how they work? Unlike most moving machines, these two don't need fuel to get them going. All they need is you!

1 When you cycle, your feet push the pedals round in a small circle. This turns a wheel called a cog, inside the chainring. The chainring usually contains two cogs, one large and one small. The cogs have teeth, and the larger the cog, the more teeth it has.

2 The chainring is connected by a chain to a second set of cogs (called the cassette) on the back wheel. The chain loops around one of the cogs in the chainring and one of the cogs in the cassette.

3 When the front cog is turned by the pedals, it pulls the chain around. This turns the rear cog, which then turns the back wheel. The front wheel is pushed along by the movement of the back wheel.

Bicycle

Want to get around your local area easily, quickly, and cheaply? Cycling is much faster than walking. And bikes don't need fuel—your muscles provide the power! Let's see how bicycles work ...

Brake lever

Brake cable

Brake arm

Gear lever

Brake block

Rear cogs

Front cogs

Cassette

Chainring

Back wheel

Chain

Pedal

Front wheel

Wheelbarrow

A wheelbarrow is made up of two simple machines: a lever and a wheel and axle. Together, they make it much easier to lift heavy loads and move them from place to place.

The wheelbarrow's wheel is the fulcrum (fixed point). The load (here it's the muddy pig!) is placed close to the wheel and the handles are farther back. The farther away the weight is from the handles, the easier it is to lift. The wheel and axle then help to move the load along.

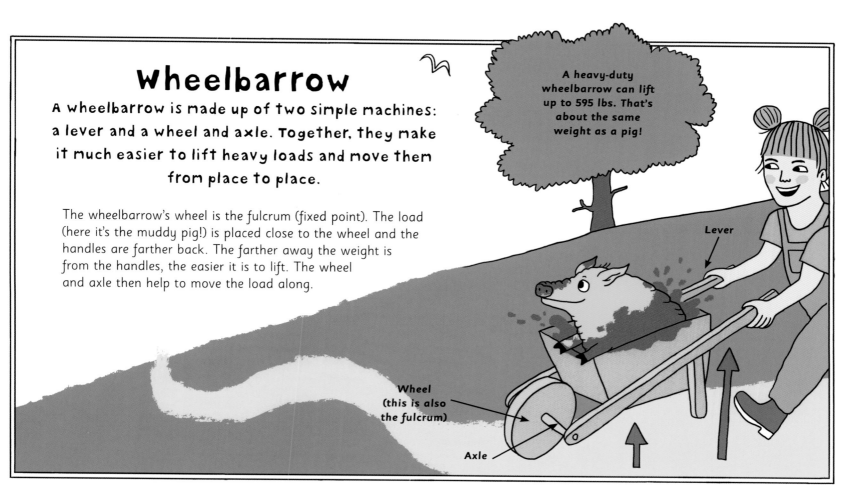

A heavy-duty wheelbarrow can lift up to 595 lbs. That's about the same weight as a pig!

Lever

Wheel (this is also the fulcrum)

Axle

BRAKES

Bike brakes are super important— they let you slow down and stop. When you squeeze the brake handle, the lever pulls a cable that squeezes the brake blocks together against the moving wheel. This makes the wheel slow down and stop.

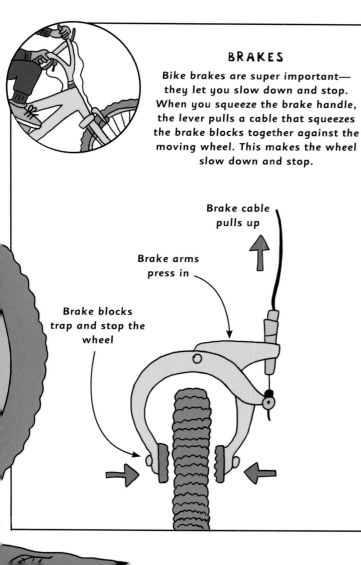

Brake cable pulls up

Brake arms press in

Brake blocks trap and stop the wheel

GEARS

The cogs in a bike are also known as gears. If you have lots of cogs, you have lots of gears. Gears help control speed and help you cycle up steep hills. When you want to shift gear, you use the gear lever on the handlebars to select the gear you'd like. The chain shifts onto the right cogs.

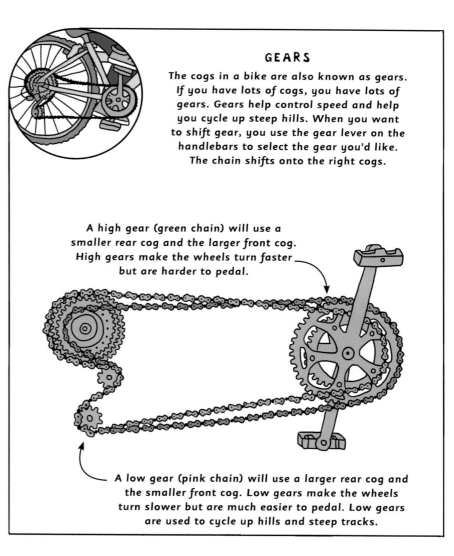

A high gear (green chain) will use a smaller rear cog and the larger front cog. High gears make the wheels turn faster but are harder to pedal.

A low gear (pink chain) will use a larger rear cog and the smaller front cog. Low gears make the wheels turn slower but are much easier to pedal. Low gears are used to cycle up hills and steep tracks.

You might be thinking "Staplers and scissors aren't machines! Why on EARTH are they in this book?" Well, they are machines, and they're actually very clever!

stapler

The first-ever stapler was made for a French king in the 1700s. Today, staplers are used in homes, schools, and offices. Do you know how they work?

1

You want to make a paper crown, and need to staple the two ends together. You put put one end over the other, and both ends between the base and head of the stapler.

2

When you press on the top of the stapler, a part called the hammer pushes the front staple downward and its points go through the two pieces of paper.

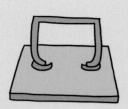

3

The bottom part of the stapler is the really clever part. It has a groove on the base. The two ends of the staple go into this groove and, because you are still pushing downward, the force makes them bend inward, neatly fastening the pieces of paper together. Hurrah! Your crown is ready for your head.

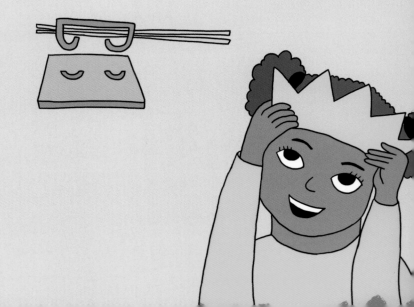

INSIDE A STAPLER

Take a look at all the pieces you would find if you took a stapler apart. Each tiny part has a job.

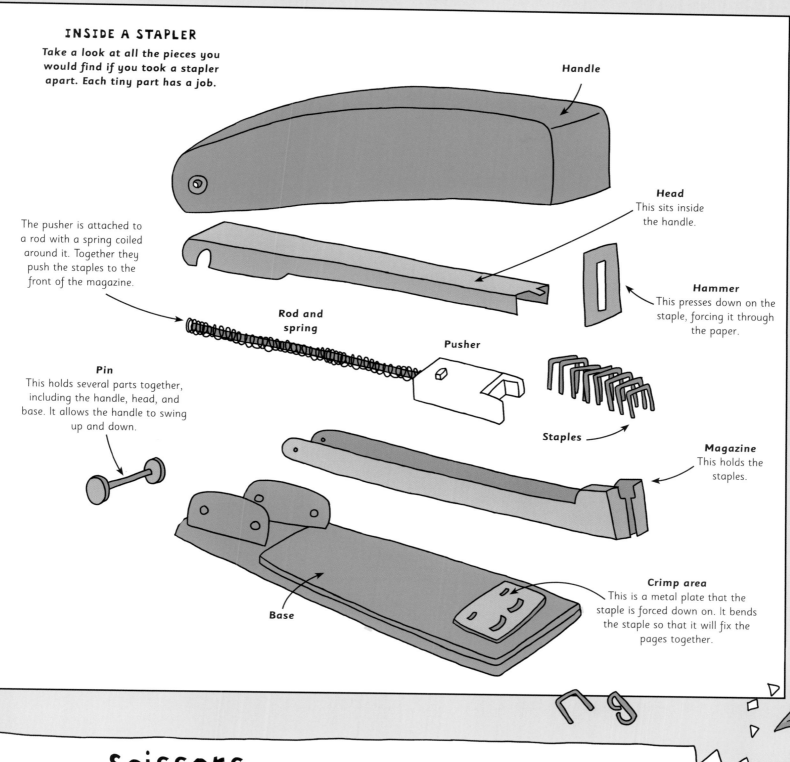

Handle

Head
This sits inside the handle.

Hammer
This presses down on the staple, forcing it through the paper.

The pusher is attached to a rod with a spring coiled around it. Together they push the staples to the front of the magazine.

Rod and spring

Pusher

Pin
This holds several parts together, including the handle, head, and base. It allows the handle to swing up and down.

Staples

Magazine
This holds the staples.

Base

Crimp area
This is a metal plate that the staple is forced down on. It bends the staple so that it will fix the pages together.

Scissors

Have you ever wondered how scissors make such neat, straight cuts?

Scissors are two machines in one—the handles are levers and the blades form a wedge. The handles join at the fulcrum. By squeezing the handles, you are pressing the levers. This creates a strong cutting force on the other side. The blades are a pair of wedges pinned together in a cross shape and they pivot around the fulcrum. They meet and cross so closely that they can cut cleanly through thin material.

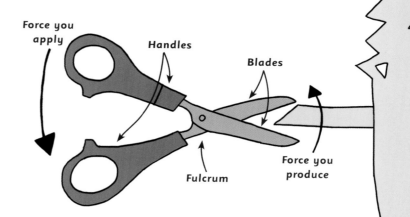

Force you apply

Handles

Blades

Fulcrum

Force you produce

KEEPING IT COOL

Refrigerators keep food cool and fresh. If you live in a hot country, you might have aircon to keep YOU cool and fresh, too. But how do these machines work? Read on and find out.

Refrigerator

Have you ever left the milk out by mistake? By the next day, it will probably have gone bad. The bacteria that make food go bad grow less quickly in cold temperatures, so refrigerators help you keep food fresh. How do they stay cold?

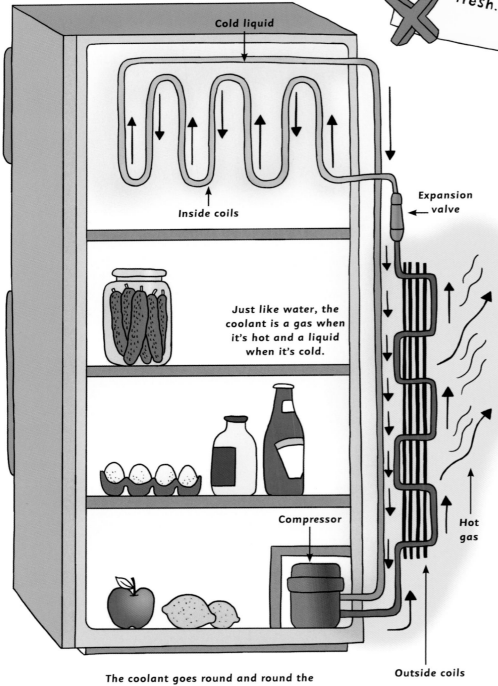

Cold liquid

Inside coils

Expansion valve

Just like water, the coolant is a gas when it's hot and a liquid when it's cold.

Compressor

Hot gas

Outside coils

The coolant goes round and round the coils, absorbing the heat from inside the fridge and taking it outside.

1 Refrigerators have a compressor, which squeezes a gas called the coolant into a small space. This makes the gas get hotter.

2 The hot gas flows into coils on the outside of the fridge. As the gas flows, it is cooled down by the air around it and turns into a liquid.

3 The liquid passes through an expansion valve, an opening that lets the liquid spread out, so it becomes colder.

4 The cold liquid flows into more coils inside the fridge. The liquid absorbs (takes in) the heat inside the fridge, making the air cold.

5 As the liquid flows through the coils, it warms up and turns back into a gas. It then goes back to the compressor, ready to start the cycle again.

Air conditioning

An air conditioner is a machine for turning your home into a giant fridge. It removes heat from inside and dumps it outside. These machines are made up of two parts, one inside the house and one outside.

4
At this point, the hot gas passes through a second set of coils and begins to lose its heat to the outside air. A second fan blows on the coils, allowing even more heat to escape outside.

3
This gas passes to the part of the machine that is outside the house. Here it passes through a compressor, where it is squeezed and made even hotter.

Compressor

Hot coils

Fan

5
The gas cools down and becomes a liquid again. This liquid passes through an expansion valve (an opening that makes the liquid spread out and become even colder.) It then enters the cold coils and begins the cycle again.

Fan

Coolant

Cold coils

Expansion valve

2
Like a refrigerator, these cold coils contain liquid coolant. As the warm air from the room flows over them, it heats the coolant inside and turns it into a gas.

1
Inside the house, warm air from the room flows into the machine. A fan blows the air over a set of cold coils and back out into the room at a cooler temperature.

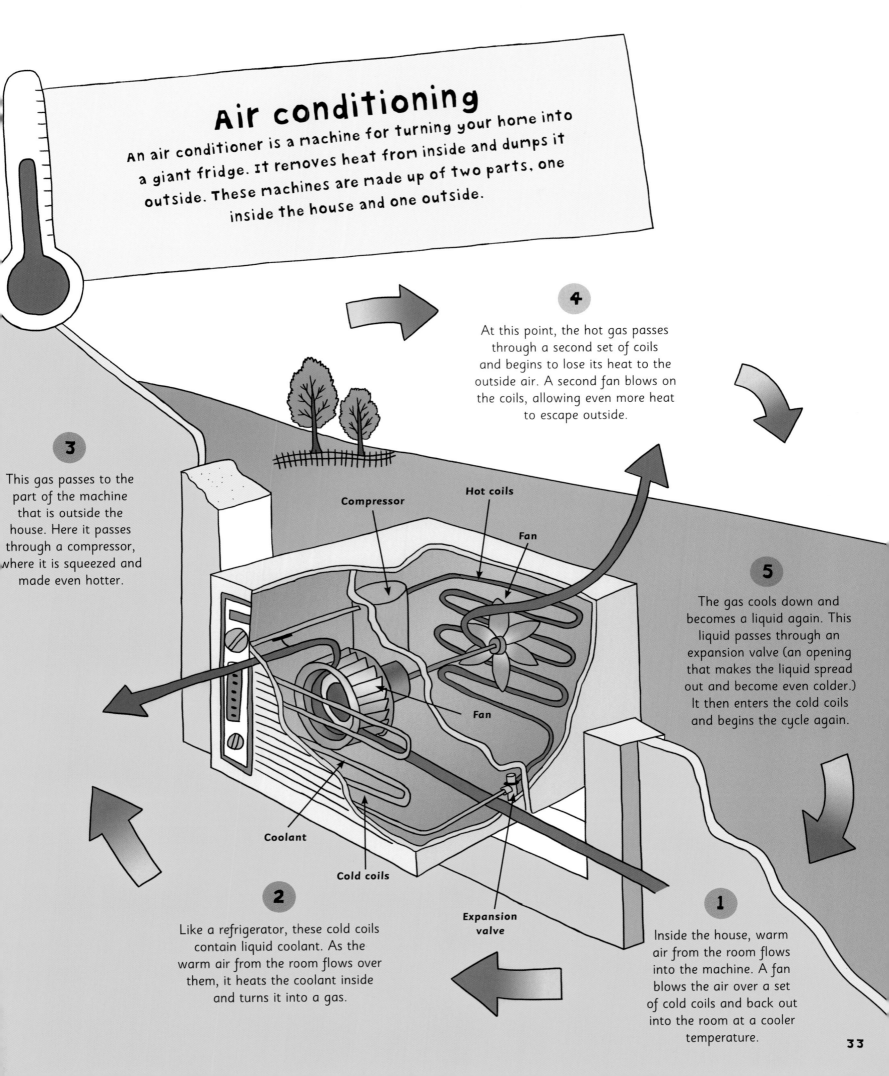

WARMING IT UP

Nothing beats being cozy and warm at home, enjoying a delicious hot meal. But have you ever stopped to wonder how your house stays toasty and food gets cooked?

Radiator

Most radiators work by using hot water to heat the air in the room. Radiators are made from metal because heat travels through most metals easily. One radiator can heat a whole room.

A radiator is long and flat so that as much of the surface as possible is in contact with the air around it.

Boiler
The boiler is a machine that heats the water.

Thermostat
The thermostat measures the temperature and tells the boiler when to switch on and off.

Pipes

Pump

1

The water is heated in a boiler and pumped through pipes to every radiator in the house.

2

Each radiator has a pipe to let the water in on one side and another to let it out on the other side. Hot water flows through the radiator and this heats up the metal surface.

3

The hot radiator heats up the air around it. Hot air always rises. As the hot air rises, there is always a flow of cooler air reaching the radiator below.

4

As the water goes through all the radiators, it slowly cools down. Pipes send the water back to the boiler to be reheated.

Microwave oven

The sun warms us naturally by sending heat to Earth using waves of energy. This is called radiation. A microwave oven uses radiation, too. It sends waves of energy to the tasty food inside.

1

You put your soup inside, set the timer, and press start. A device called a magnetron then turns the electricity into wave energy and fires these waves at a spinning fan.

2

The waves bounce across the cooking area to the metal sides, which reflect them back.

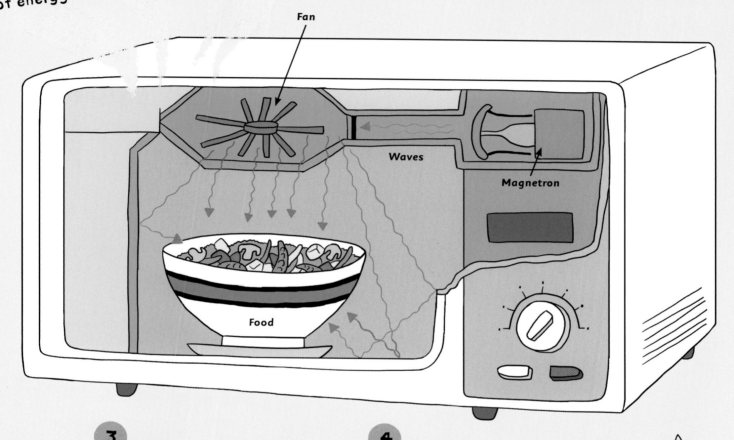

Fan

Waves

Magnetron

Food

3

A rotating dish turns the food round and round to make sure the waves reach every part.

4

The waves make all the water molecules in the soup shake and rub against other molecules. When things rub against each other, they heat up. Ping! Time's up—your soup is ready to slurp.

PERCY SPENCER (1894-1970)

In the 1940s, during World War II, US engineer Percy Spencer was working on radar, a system using radio waves to find out the position of ships and planes. One day, he was standing next to a magnetron when he noticed that a chocolate bar in his pocket had melted. He realized that the waves from the magnetron could cook food. After Spencer's lucky accident, he invented the first microwave oven.

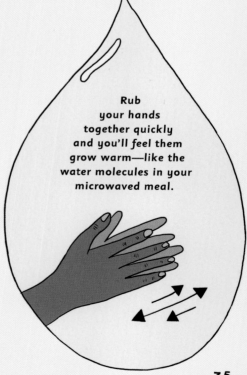

Rub your hands together quickly and you'll feel them grow warm—like the water molecules in your microwaved meal.

MACHINES FOR FUN

Have you ever wondered how some of your favorite toys actually work? Take a look at the science behind these fun machines.

Radio-controlled toy

It's your birthday and you've been given a radio-controlled car. You have great fun playing with it, but how exactly does it work?

1 Your car has a hand-held controller, which has a lever to turn the car left or right and another to go forward or backward. It also has an antenna. When you press the lever, two wires inside the controller are pushed together.

Antenna

2 This completes an electrical circuit, which creates an electrical signal. A transmitter, inside the controller, picks up the signal and turns it to radio waves. The antenna then sends the radio waves out to the car several thousand times a second. The radio waves pass on information such as which direction the car should drive in.

Antenna

3 The radio waves are picked up by an antenna on the car, which then sends them to a circuit board inside the car.

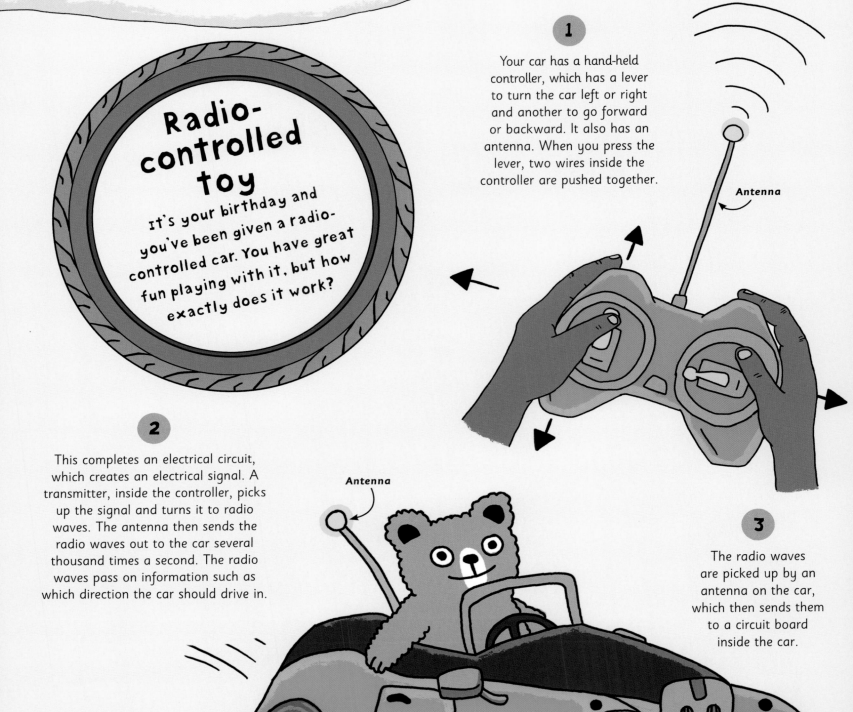

Pogo stick

A pogo stick uses the stored energy of a spring.

1

A pogo stick contains a spring mechanism. When you step on it, your weight presses down the spring. This compresses (squeezes) the spring, which absorbs and stores the energy from you stepping on it. This means it is now full of energy waiting to be released.

2

As soon as you start to move upward, the spring can expand, which releases the energy, giving you a push upward. Whooa!

4

A microchip (a tiny computer) on the circuit board recognizes the pattern of the radio waves and works out the instruction. The microchip then sends a charge from the battery in the car to the right motor. There are usually two motors: one motor turns the front wheels left or right and the other makes the back wheels spin forward or backward. Time to take teddy for a drive!

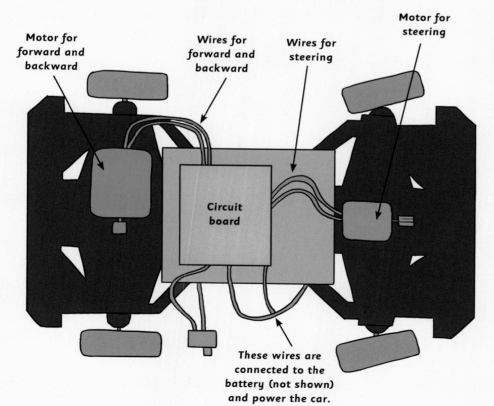

Motor for forward and backward

Wires for forward and backward

Wires for steering

Motor for steering

Circuit board

These wires are connected to the battery (not shown) and power the car.

HOW A BATTERY WORKS

A battery has two ends: one positive, marked with a '+' and one negative, which is marked with a '-'. At the negative end, tiny particles called electrons gather. These electrons try to move to the positive end but they can't travel through the battery. If you create a circuit by connecting a wire to the two ends of the battery, the electrons can flow through that instead. This movement of electrons creates electricity that can power motors and other electrical devices.

MACHINES TO KEEP YOU SAFE

Some of the most important machines are those that keep us safe. Alarms warn us of danger, and locks and keys keep us and our homes safe from harm. But how do these everyday saviors work?

smoke alarm

A smoke alarm is fixed to the ceiling because smoke rises. This alarm uses a light beam to quickly warn of smoke from a fire.

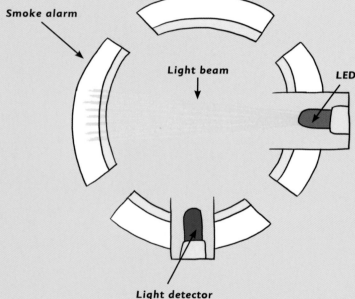

Smoke alarm

Light beam

LED

Light detector

1

Inside the smoke alarm, a device called an LED (light-emitting diode) makes a beam of light every 10 seconds. The light travels in a straight line and does not reach the light detector.

2

If there is smoke in the room, for instance if you've burnt your breakfast, it rises and enters the smoke alarm through the openings in the sides.

3

When the smoke enters, the light is scattered. Some of the light reaches the light detector.

4

The light detector sends a signal to an electrical circuit. Electricity flows around the circuit and sets off the alarm.

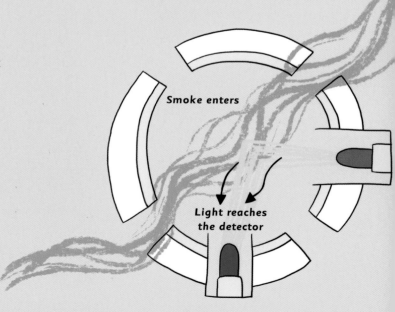

Smoke enters

Light reaches the detector

door lock

Turn the right key in a lock and it opens. Use the wrong key and the lock won't budge! One of the most common types of lock is a cylinder lock. These locks are often used in front doors and padlocks. To open one, you just have to turn the cylinder—but it's not as simple as it sounds! Let's take a look.

1

Inside the cylinder are two sets of pins of varying lengths. The red pins sit above the blue pins. Springs push the red pins down into the cylinder and hold them there so the cylinder will not turn.

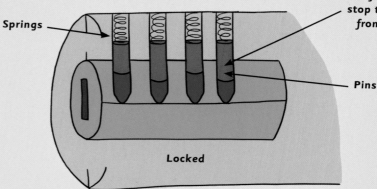

Springs

The four red pins stop the cylinder from turning.

Pins

Locked

2

To turn the cylinder, we use a key. The right key has jagged points that are exactly the right length to push the red pins up and out of the cylinder.

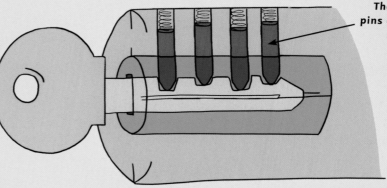

The key pushes the pins out of the cylinder, so it can turn.

We've been using door locks for quite a while. The Ancient Egyptians made the first locks around 6,000 years ago!

3

Now none of the pins are stopping the cylinder from turning. The key can turn the cylinder, which pulls the lock out of the door so that it can open.

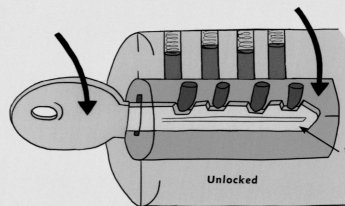

The key can now turn the cylinder and unlock the door.

Unlocked

MACHINES UP HIGH

Look up at a construction site and you'll see cranes of all different sizes. Some tower into the skies and help to build skyscrapers. Others are smaller but still stretch higher than most houses and lift enormous loads. How do they work? Let's find out!

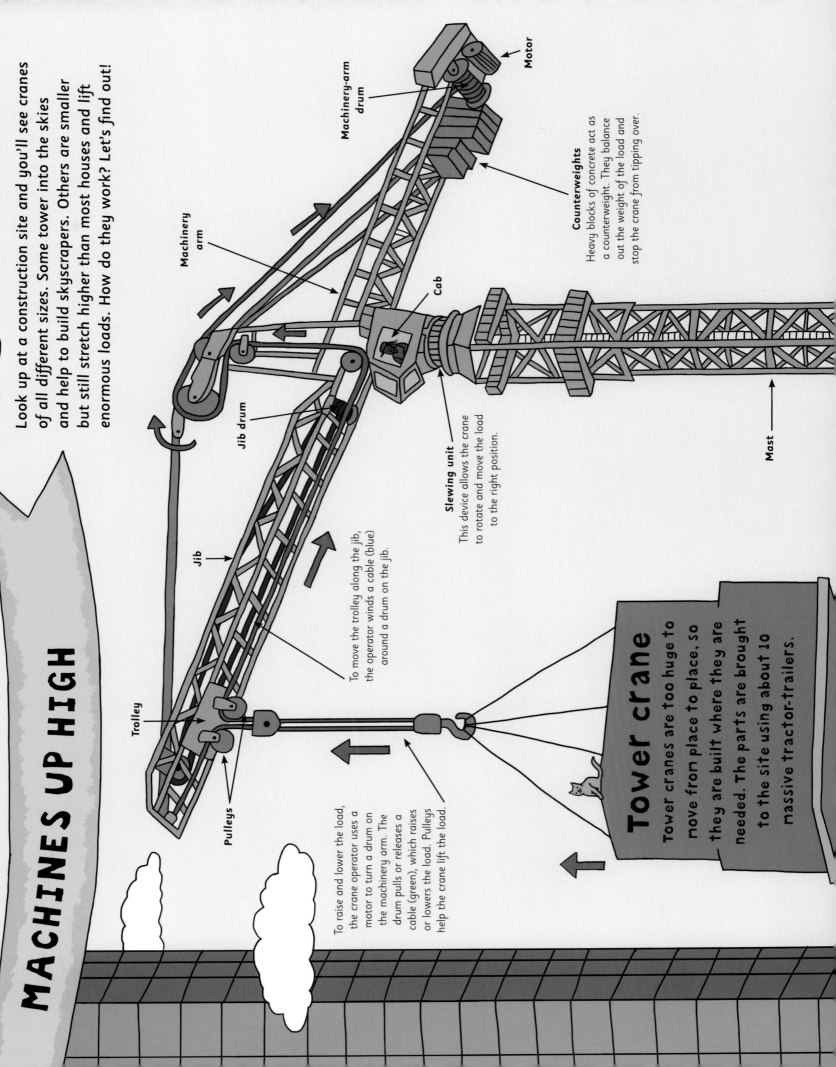

Motor

Machinery-arm drum

Machinery arm

Cab

Counterweights
Heavy blocks of concrete act as a counterweight. They balance out the weight of the load and stop the crane from tipping over.

Slewing unit
This device allows the crane to rotate and move the load to the right position.

Jib drum

Jib

Mast

To move the trolley along the jib, the operator winds a cable (blue) around a drum on the jib.

Trolley

To raise and lower the load, the crane operator uses a motor to turn a drum on the machinery arm. The drum pulls or releases a cable (green), which raises or lowers the load. Pulleys help the crane lift the load.

Pulleys

Tower crane
Tower cranes are too huge to move from place to place, so they are built where they are needed. The parts are brought to the site using about 10 massive tractor-trailers.

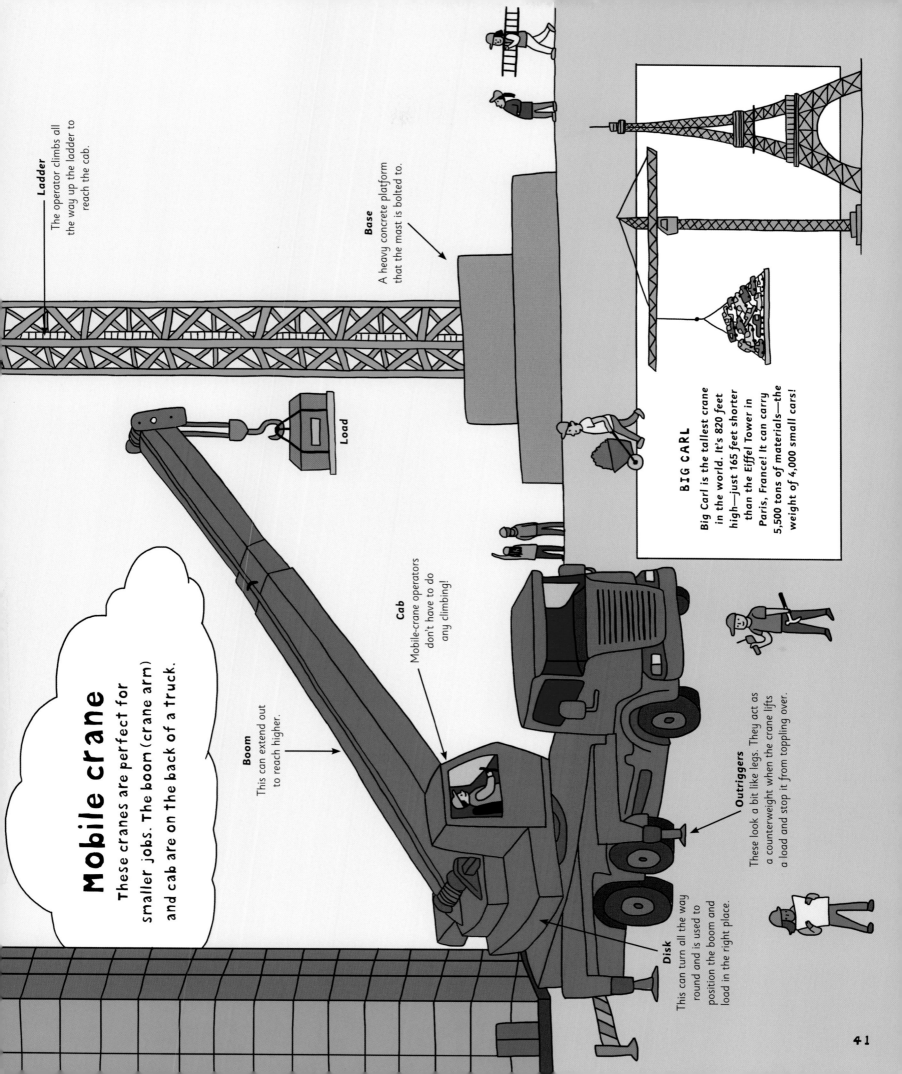

Mobile crane

These cranes are perfect for smaller jobs. The boom (crane arm) and cab are on the back of a truck.

Ladder
The operator climbs all the way up the ladder to reach the cab.

Base
A heavy concrete platform that the mast is bolted to.

Load

Cab
Mobile-crane operators don't have to do any climbing!

Boom
This can extend out to reach higher.

Outriggers
These look a bit like legs. They act as a counterweight when the crane lifts a load and stop it from toppling over.

Disk
This can turn all the way round and is used to position the boom and load in the right place.

BIG CARL

Big Carl is the tallest crane in the world. It's 820 feet high—just 165 feet shorter than the Eiffel Tower in Paris, France! It can carry 5,500 tons of materials—the weight of 4,000 small cars!

41

THE BIG ONE

There are some truly enormous machines but few people have ever seen them. At nearly 17 miles long, the Large Hadron Collider is the biggest machine in the world. It is hidden away 330 feet underground in Switzerland at a scientific research organization called CERN.

Beams of particles are first sent through the Super Proton Synchrotron to accelerate their speed. They then pass into the Collider (an enormous, round tunnel) where they are sent racing around in opposite directions.

The particles are guided around the tunnel by a magnetic field created by over 1,200 electromagnets (pieces of metal that become magnetic when electricity goes through them) that line the walls of the tunnel. Each magnet is 50 feet long and weighs about 39 tons!

The particles collide—crash into each other— at almost the speed of light. There are 1 billion collisions every second! When the particles collide, they split into even smaller particles called subatomic particles.

These collisions happen in four different places in the tunnel. Detectors collect data and send it up to computers and scientists above ground. The scientists then use the data to try to solve some of the mysteries of science. Some are searching for specific particles or new particles while others are trying to find out more about the Big Bang.

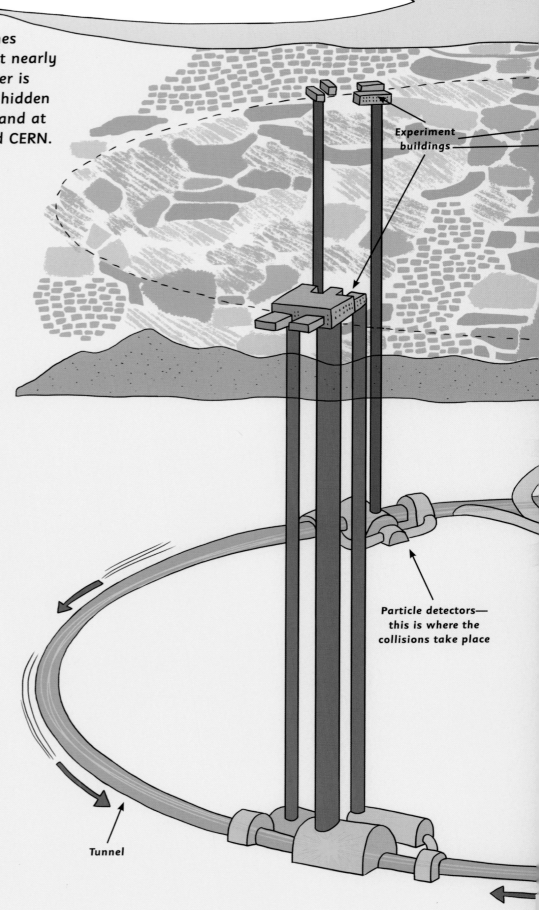

Experiment buildings

Particle detectors— this is where the collisions take place

Tunnel

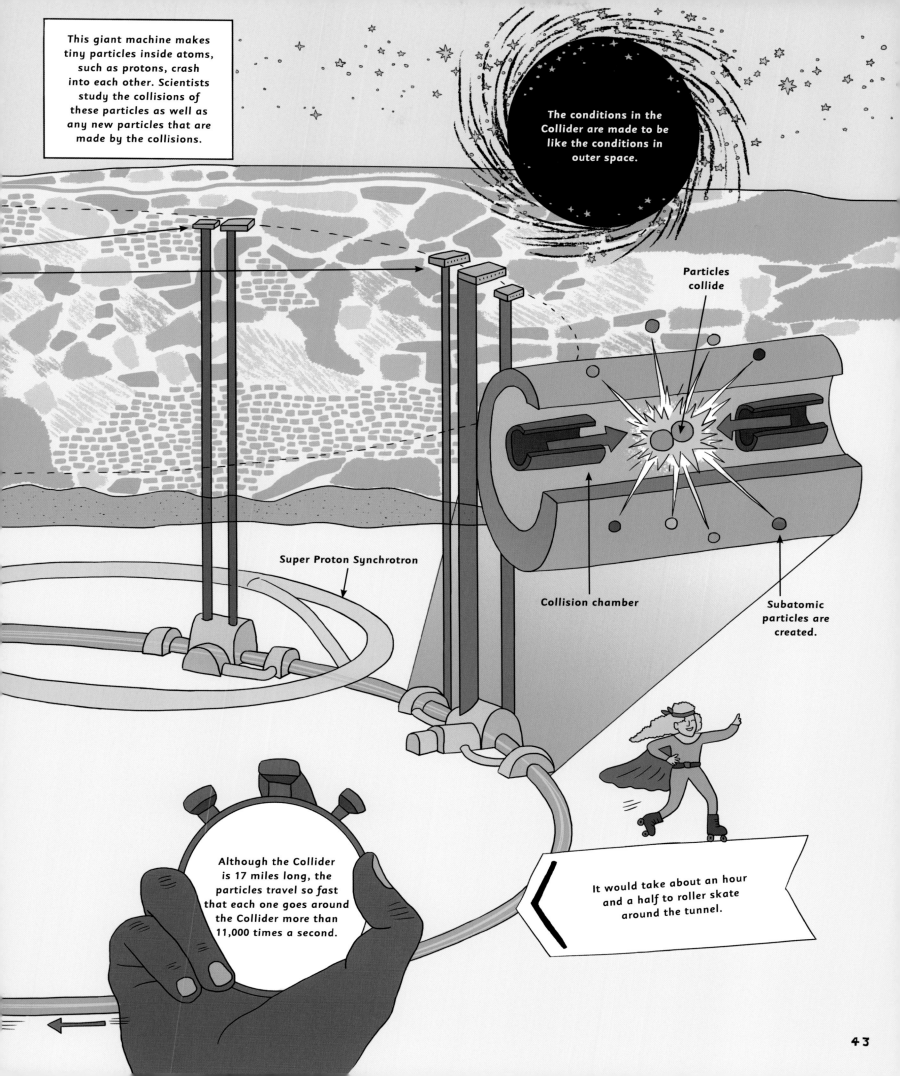

This giant machine makes tiny particles inside atoms, such as protons, crash into each other. Scientists study the collisions of these particles as well as any new particles that are made by the collisions.

The conditions in the Collider are made to be like the conditions in outer space.

Particles collide

Super Proton Synchrotron

Collision chamber

Subatomic particles are created.

Although the Collider is 17 miles long, the particles travel so fast that each one goes around the Collider more than 11,000 times a second.

It would take about an hour and a half to roller skate around the tunnel.

ROBOTS

In stories, robots are often machines that act a bit like humans and are super intelligent. In real life, robots are machines that can do complicated jobs.

Mars Rover

We might not have sent a human to Mars yet, but we still know a lot about the planet, thanks to the incredible Mars Rover robots. So how do scientists control the robots from Earth—about 140 million miles away from Mars?

Satellite

Earth

Mars Rover

Mars

The Rover even has a laser so it can blast rocks apart to find out what they are made of.

A camera takes photos to send back to Earth.

1

NASA (the space agency that invented and owns the Mars Rovers) sends commands to the robots using satellites. An antenna on Earth sends a signal to a satellite orbiting Mars. The satellite then sends the signal on to the Rover.

2

The Rover's antenna picks up the commands, which tell it where to go and which experiments to do.

An onboard mini-laboratory examines the samples.

3

The Rover then carries out the commands and gathers all the information. Later, it sends the data back to Earth using satellite signals.

Strong wheels help the Rover to travel over Mars' rough surface.

The Rover uses its robot arm to collect rock samples.

Machines that make machines

Every year, robots help to produce millions of cars. They can do the same work over and over again without ever getting tired. And they never complain!

In a car factory, the cars move along a production line and as they do, different robots carry out different tasks.

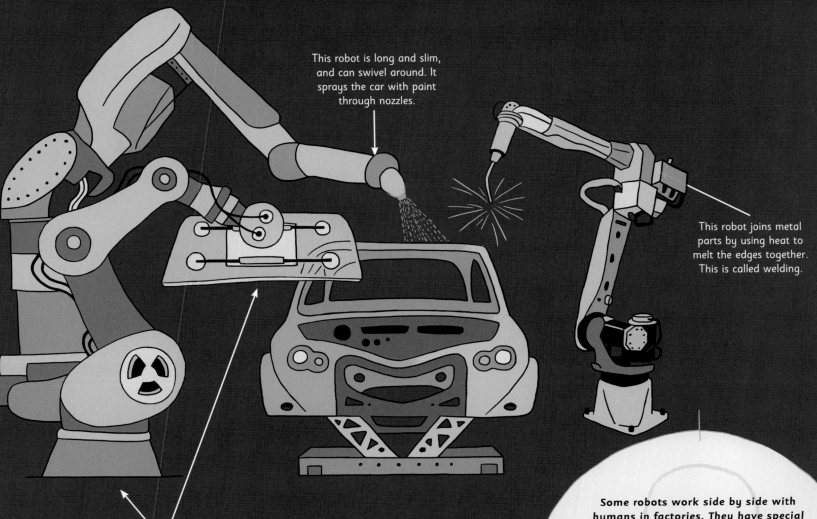

This robot is long and slim, and can swivel around. It sprays the car with paint through nozzles.

This robot joins metal parts by using heat to melt the edges together. This is called welding.

This robot has suckers on the end of its arm to hold the windshield while it finds the right position. Then it places the windshield in the car.

Some robots work side by side with humans in factories. They have special machine-vision systems to make sure they don't accidentally bump into their workmates.

45

GLOSSARY

antenna
A piece of equipment made of wire for receiving or sending radio and television signals

atom
The smallest part of an element that can exist. An element is a substance that is only made up of one kind of atom, such as carbon.

axle
A rod fixed to the middle of a wheel

circuit
The loop of wires and equipment along which an electric current flows

circuit board
The board that holds electrical circuits inside an electrical device

collision
When two things crash into each other

combustion
Burning

compressor
A machine that compresses air or other gases

conductor
A substance that allows electricity to pass through it

counterweight
On a crane, a weight that is equal to one on the other side, so the crane balances

current
The flow of electricity

cylinder
An object with round ends and long straight sides

digital
Using a system of receiving and sending information as a series of ones and zeros—this is how computers work

force
A pushing or pulling action that can make things move, change direction, or change shape. If you kick a ball, the force from your foot makes it fly upward. When the wind blows, its force makes the blades of a wind turbine turn round and round.

friction
The action of one object or surface moving against another

fulcrum
The point on which a lever turns or is supported. For example, the wheel is the fulcrum that supports the load of a wheelbarrow.

gear
A device that changes the speed of a machine or vehicle

generator
A machine for producing electricity

hull
The bottom part of a ship, which goes in the water

laser
A device that makes a powerful beam of light that can cut metal and be used in operations

lever
A bar or board that rests on a fulcrum. It can be used to lift something by placing one end under an object and pushing down or pulling up the other end.

mechanical energy
Machines use mechanical energy to do work. When you get on your bike and raise your foot, it has potential (stored) energy. When you press your foot on the pedal, the potential energy becomes kinetic energy. The wheels go round and the bike moves.

microchip
A tiny computer on a circuit board, the board that holds electrical circuits inside an electrical device

motor
A device that uses electricity or gas to make a machine or a vehicle work

orbit
A curved path that a planet or object follows as it moves around a planet or star

particle
A tiny piece of matter, such as a photon, an electron, or a proton, which is part of an atom

piston
A part of an engine. It is a short cylinder inside a tube that moves up and down or backward and forward to make other parts of the engine move.

pressure
The force or weight with which something presses against something else

pulley
A wheel with a rope looped around its edge, used to make it easier to lift objects

radiation
The transfer of energy from one place to another in the form of waves or particles. Heat, light, sound, and X-rays are all examples of radiation

radio wave
A low-energy wave used for communicating over long distances

satellite
An electronic device that is sent into space and moves around the Earth (or another planet). It is used for communicating by radio and television and for providing information.

scanner
A device for recording or checking something, or looking inside people's bodies. It uses light, sound, or X-rays.

sensor
A device that reacts to light, heat, or pressure to make a machine do something or show something

shaft
The long, narrow part of a tool or machine

transformer
A device for reducing or increasing the voltage of an electric power supply

vibrate
To shake from side to side very quickly

voltage
The amount of electrical force

wedge
A simple machine with a thick and a thin end that can be used to split objects in two

FURTHER READING

MORE MACHINES

What Do Machines Do All Day?
By Jo Nelson and Aleksander Savic
Wide Eyed Editions, 2019

What on Earth? Robots
By Jenny Fretland VanVoorst
and Paulina Morgan
QEB Publishing, 2018

How Things Work: Inside Out
National Geographic Kids, 2017

INVENTORS AND INVENTIONS

The Story of Inventions
By Catherine Barr, Steve Williams and
Amy Husband
Frances Lincoln Children's Books, 2020

100 Inventions That Made History
DK Children, 2014

SEE THE WORLD IN A NEW WAY

The Everyday Journeys of Ordinary Things
By Libby Deutsch and Valpuri Kerttula
Ivy Kids, 2019

Supersize Cross Sections: Inside Engines
By Pascale Hedelin and Lou Rhin
Wide Eyed Editions, 2019

The Book of Comparisons
By Clive Gifford and Paul Boston
Ivy Kids, 2018

**In Focus: 101 Close Ups,
Cross-sections and Cutaways**
By Libby Walden
360 Degrees, 2016

SCIENCE AND ENGINEERING

What Do Scientists Do All Day?
By Jane Wilsher and Maggie Li
Wide Eyed Editions, 2020

Excellent Engineering
By Rob Beattie and Sam Peet
QED Publishing, 2019

Scientist Academy
By Steve Martin and Essi Kimpimäki
Ivy Kids, 2017

DKfindout! Engineering
DK Children, 2017